FRANCIS FRITH'S

GUISBOROUGH
PHOTOGRAPHIC MEMORIES

THE FRANCIS FRITH COLLECTION

www.francisfrith.com

FRANCIS FRITH'S

GUISBOROUGH

PHOTOGRAPHIC MEMORIES

ROGER DARNTON is a partner in a leading independent estate agents in Guisborough. A native of the town and a member of a long established Guisborough family, Roger has always been passionate about his home town; he is dedicated to ensuring that its social and photographic history is recorded and preserved for the enjoyment of both present and future generations. He was the founder of the Guisborough Museum, of which he now serves as Chairman and Honorary Curator and in 2004 was nominated as Guisborough's "citizen of the year" for his service to the town. Roger is married to Jackie, has one son, Tim, and lives at the family home in Guisborough where he was born.

FRANCIS FRITH'S
PHOTOGRAPHIC MEMORIES

GUISBOROUGH

PHOTOGRAPHIC MEMORIES

ROGER DARNTON

First published in the United Kingdom in 2004 by
Frith Book Company Ltd

This edition published exclusively for
The Guisborough Book Shop

Paperback Edition 2004
ISBN 1-85937-933-8

British Library Cataloguing in Publication Data

Francis Frith's Guisborough - Photographic Memories
Roger Darnton
ISBN 1-85937-933-8

Frith Book Company Ltd
Frith's Barn, Teffont,
Salisbury, Wiltshire SP3 5QP
Tel: +44 (0) 1722 716 376
Email: info@francisfrith.co.uk
www.francisfrith.co.uk

Printed and bound in Great Britain

Front Cover: **GUISBOROUGH**, *Westgate 1899* 44758t
Frontispiece: **GUISBOROUGH**, *Market Place 1891* 29209

*The colour-tinting is for illustrative purposes only, and is not intended
to be historically accurate*

AS WITH ANY HISTORICAL DATABASE THE FRITH ARCHIVE IS
CONSTANTLY BEING CORRECTED AND IMPROVED AND THE
PUBLISHERS WOULD WELCOME INFORMATION ON OMISSIONS OR
INACCURACIES

CONTENTS

FRANCIS FRITH
VICTORIAN PIONEER

FRANCIS FRITH, founder of the world-famous photographic archive, was a complex and multi-talented man. A devout Quaker and a highly successful Victorian businessman, he was philosophical by nature and pioneering in outlook.

By 1855 he had already established a wholesale grocery business in Liverpool, and sold it for the astonishing sum of £200,000, which is the equivalent today of over £15,000,000. Now a very rich man, he was able to indulge his passion for travel. As a child he had pored over travel books written by early explorers, and his fancy and imagination had been stirred by family holidays to the sublime mountain regions of Wales and Scotland. 'What lands of spirit-stirring and enriching scenes and places!' he had written. He was to return to these scenes of grandeur in later years to 'recapture the thousands of vivid and tender memories', but with a different purpose. Now in his thirties, and captivated by the new science of photography, Frith set out on a series of pioneering journeys up the Nile and to the Near East that occupied him from 1856 until 1860.

INTRIGUE AND EXPLORATION

These far-flung journeys were packed with intrigue and adventure. In his life story, written when he was sixty-three, Frith tells of being held captive by bandits, and of fighting 'an awful midnight battle to the very point of surrender with a deadly pack of hungry, wild dogs'. Wearing flowing Arab costume, Frith arrived at Akaba by camel sixty years before Lawrence of Arabia, where he encountered 'desert princes and rival sheikhs, blazing with jewel-hilted swords'.

He was the first photographer to venture beyond the sixth cataract of the Nile. Africa was still the mysterious 'Dark Continent', and Stanley and Livingstone's historic meeting was a decade into the future. The conditions for picture taking confound belief. He laboured for hours in his wicker dark-room in the sweltering heat of the desert, while the volatile chemicals fizzed dangerously in their trays. Back in London he exhibited his photographs and was 'rapturously cheered' by members of the Royal Society. His reputation as a photographer was made overnight.

VENTURE OF A LIFE-TIME

Characteristically, Frith quickly spotted the opportunity to create a new business as a specialist publisher of photographs. He lived in an era of immense and sometimes violent change.

For the poor in the early part of Victoria's reign work was exhausting and the hours long, and people had precious little free time to enjoy themselves. Most had no transport other than a cart or gig at their disposal, and rarely travelled far beyond the boundaries of their own town or village. However, by the 1870s the railways had threaded their way across the country, and Bank Holidays and half-day Saturdays had been made obligatory by Act of Parliament. All of a sudden the working man and his family were able to enjoy days out and see a little more of the world.

With typical business acumen, Francis Frith foresaw that these new tourists would enjoy having souvenirs to commemorate their days out. In 1860 he married Mary Ann Rosling and set out on a new career: his aim was to photograph every city, town and village in Britain. For the next thirty years he travelled the country by train and by pony and trap, producing fine photographs of seaside resorts and beauty spots that were keenly bought by millions of Victorians. These prints were painstakingly pasted into family albums and pored over during the dark nights of winter, rekindling precious memories of summer excursions.

THE RISE OF FRITH & CO

Frith's studio was soon supplying retail shops all over the country. To meet the demand he gathered about him a small team of photographers, and published the work of independent artist-photographers of the calibre of Roger Fenton and Francis Bedford. In order to gain some understanding of the scale of Frith's business one only has to look at the catalogue issued by Frith & Co in 1886: it runs to some 670 pages, listing not only many thousands of views of the British Isles but also many photographs of most European countries, and China, Japan, the USA and Canada - note the sample page shown on page 9 from the hand-written Frith & Co ledgers recording the pictures. By 1890 Frith had created the greatest specialist photographic publishing company in the world, with over 2,000 sales outlets - more than the combined number that Boots and WH Smith have today! The picture on the next page shows the Frith & Co display board at Ingleton in the Yorkshire Dales (left of window). Beautifully constructed with a mahogany frame and gilt inserts, it could display up to a dozen local scenes.

POSTCARD BONANZA

The ever-popular holiday postcard we know today took many years to develop. In 1870 the Post Office issued the first plain cards, with a pre-printed stamp on one face. In 1894 they allowed other publishers' cards to be sent through the mail with an attached adhesive halfpenny stamp. Demand grew rapidly, and in 1895 a new size of postcard was permitted called the court card, but there was little room for illustration. In 1899, a year after Frith's death, a new card measuring 5.5 x 3.5 inches became the standard format, but it was not until 1902 that the divided back came into being, so that the address and message could be on one face and a full-size illustration on the other. Frith & Co were in the vanguard of postcard development: Frith's sons Eustace and Cyril continued their father's monumental task, expanding the number of views offered to the public and recording more and more places in Britain, as the coasts and countryside were opened up to mass travel.

Francis Frith had died in 1898 at his villa in Cannes, his great project still growing. The archive he created continued in business for another seventy years. By 1970 it contained over a third of a million pictures showing 7,000 British towns and villages.

FRANCIS FRITH'S LEGACY

Frith's legacy to us today is of immense significance and value, for the magnificent archive of evocative photographs he created provides a unique record of change in the cities, towns and villages throughout Britain over a century and more. Frith and his fellow studio photographers revisited locations many times down the years to update their views, compiling for us an enthralling and colourful pageant of British life and character.

We are fortunate that Frith was dedicated to recording the minutiae of everyday life. For it is this sheer wealth of visual data, the painstaking chronicle of changes in dress, transport, street layouts, buildings, housing, engineering and landscape that captivates us so much today. His remarkable images offer us a powerful link with the past and with the lives of our ancestors.

THE VALUE OF THE ARCHIVE TODAY

Computers have now made it possible for Frith's many thousands of images to be accessed almost instantly. Frith's images are increasingly used as visual resources, by social historians, by researchers into genealogy and ancestry, by architects and town planners, and by teachers involved in local history projects.

In addition, the archive offers every one of us an opportunity to examine the places where we and our families have lived and worked down the years. Highly successful in Frith's own era, the archive is now, a century and more on, entering a new phase of popularity. Historians consider the Francis Frith Collection to be of prime national importance. It is the only archive of its kind remaining in private ownership. Francis Frith's archive is now housed in an historic timber barn in the beautiful village of Teffont in Wiltshire. Its founder would not recognize the archive office as it is today. In place of the many thousands of dusty boxes containing glass plate negatives and an all-pervading odour of photographic chemicals, there are now ranks of computer screens. He would be amazed to watch his images travelling round the world at unimaginable speeds through internet lines.

The archive's future is both bright and exciting. Francis Frith, with his unshakeable belief in making photographs available to the greatest number of people, would undoubtedly approve of what is being done today with his lifetime's work. His photographs depicting our shared past are now bringing pleasure and enlightenment to millions around the world a century and more after his death.

GUISBOROUGH
AN INTRODUCTION

GUISBOROUGH'S NAME suggests that it was originally a fortified town. At the time of the Domesday Book, the town was known as 'Ghigesburg' or 'Gighesborc'; the 'borough' element implies a fortified place, while the first element is a rare Norse personal name, 'Gigr'. Thus it is possible that there may have been an early fort of either English or Roman date here known as 'Gigr's Fort'.

It is undeniably the case that one of Guisborough's greatest charms has always been its location nestled in a valley between the Cleveland and Eston Hills. Earlier historians long since identified the individuality of the town as being its compact secluded situation 'pleasantly set among hills and thriving on its own resources'. Despite the ravages of modern housing estates and road networks,

GUISBOROUGH, *Westgate 1899* 44758

Guisborough still retains the strong imprint of its centuries of past history, and the atmosphere observed and enjoyed by earlier generations can still be evoked in the 21st century. The town is ringed by a small stream known locally as Chapel Beck, which to the north becomes Howl Beck and to the west is joined by Hutton Beck. The high landscape value of the Guisborough area is reinforced by its adjoining the North Yorkshire Moors National Park immediately to the south. The hill slopes to this side of the town have long provided scenic walks for the residents of Guisborough, who have witnessed a pattern of timber cutting during the First World War, replanting by the Forestry Commission and now, in the 21st century, another programme of tree felling, which is revealing again the contours of the hills' southern escarpments.

As to the shape of the town as we know it today, much can be explained by its apparent Roman origins. The respected historian Dr Elgee considered that the Roman fort suggested by the name of the town was situated in the modern centre of Guisborough, and that the Market Place and the four routes radiating from it, Northgate, Westgate, Church Street and Belmangate, follow the general plan of roads coming from a Roman station. This theory is reinforced by the discovery here of Roman coins and a brass helmet, now in the British Museum.

Without doubt one of the greatest influences on the shape and development of Guisborough was the priory. Founded in 1119, Guisborough Priory was the earliest and most important Augustinian priory in the country, and was dedicated to Saint Mary. Robert de Brus the second, whose family had vast land holdings in the north of England, gave generously in land, money and the granting of tithes, ensuring the priory's wealth and growth. Today in the town's parish church of St Nicholas we have a permanent reminder of the influence of the de Brus family in the De Brus Cenotaph, which commemorates the five de Brus's of Skelton and five de Brus's of

GUISBOROUGH, *Market Place 1907* 58660

11

Annandale, descendents of the priory's founder. As the priory developed, other land was chartered to it; by the time of the Dissolution, it held virtually all of Guisborough and was the fourth richest monastery in Yorkshire.

The Augustinian order at the priory were canons regular (in other words, they lived in obedience to the rule of St Augustine); they were known as black canons because of their habits of long black cassocks and hoods. These gave rise to the local legend of a black monk reputed to haunt the priory ruins and charged with guarding treasure left by the monks as they fled at the time of the Dissolution. Although little remains of the priory church today, the magnificent proportions of the great east window testifies to the imposing character of the former structure. It is hard to visualise in the 21st century, but a visit to Ripon Cathedral gives some impression of how Guisborough Priory must have looked: Ripon is built in the same Decorated style, and has an east end bearing many similarities to Guisborough. However, Guisborough had one of the largest east windows of this period, and Guisborough Priory was considered 'a landmark in the development of northern Gothic architecture'. The original building of 1119 was almost destroyed by fire in 1289, and to this day charred stonework can be seen on the bases of the ruined nave columns, which were retained in the rebuilding programme of the 14th century.

The Dissolution of the Monasteries under Henry VIII brought this important chapter in the history of Guisborough to an end. The Dissolution Survey of 1539 showed that Guisborough had 250 houses and a population of between 1000 and 1250. Nearly all the inhabitants were tenants of the priory; 80% of them had cottages but no gardens, and the rest had a little land (under 10 acres each). This seems to reflect the absence of a wealthier class of merchants or craftsmen of the kind which existed in the true boroughs of North Yorkshire, where they had been allowed more preferential terms of

GUISBOROUGH, *Westgate c1960* G66053

12

tenure than existed in Guisborough – this shows that the priory had a strong influence on the social development of the town at this period. As to the fate of the priory church building, a walk around some of the older parts of the town today gives us our answer. The immediate successors of the priors, forbears of the present-day Chaloner family, let out the priory buildings as a 'quarry', and so many of the 16th-, 17th- and 18th-century buildings of the town incorporate priory stone.

The holding of a market has always been synonymous with Guisborough; this again is linked to the priory, as a grant of 1263 gave permission for a weekly market and an annual fair lasting three days. This was probably held on a large area in front of the priory gate and the parish church. The parish church itself, always independent of its immediate neighbour the priory church, has stood on its present site since at least the time of the Domesday Book; the earliest parts of the existing structure date from the 16th century.

The street plan of the present-day town centre is heavily influenced by the medieval pattern of land holding. The curved medieval strips running between Westgate and the north and south back lanes (present-day Bolckow Street/Park Lane and Rectory Lane) were passed from one generation to another, and during the late 19th and 20th century, speculative builders developed the area literally strip by strip. Whilst today Westgate forms the heart of the town, Westgate is not actually mentioned by name until 1549; before this it was simply a track running on an east/west orientation through the strips, which ran north to south. The supposition is that with the ensuing growth of Guisborough's population and commercial life, Westgate developed as we know it today. The antiquity of Northgate is not in any doubt, for it was part of 'Wiltungate', the main road from Wilton and the Tees to Guisborough. In contrast to its role in later centuries, Belmangate, which lies to the south of Westgate, was undoubtedly the most important

GUISBOROUGH, *Market Place 1891* 29210

street in the town in the 12th century. Until the building of the railway station in 1854, it was separate from the rest of the town, and indeed there are a number of references to its being 'a hamlet attached to Guisborough'. Centuries of heavy traffic and its importance as the southern exit to the town explain its picturesque sunken nature; it was the main road from Guisborough to the south, ie Malton and York.

The closure of Guisborough Priory and the passing of the priory's lands to Thomas Chaloner, an influential figure in royal circles during the mid 16th century, marks the beginning of another important chapter in Guisborough's history. The Chaloner family have remained interwoven with the development of the town since this time. Their first significant influence on the town was in 1595, when Thomas Chaloner the second founded an alum mine at Belman Bank on the southern side of Guisborough. Although the enterprise prospered (it was Britain's first successful alum

mine) it did not notably increase the population or alter the physical shape of the town.

From the mid 16th to the mid 19th century, Guisborough saw very little change or development. Being principally an agricultural community with a weekly market, Guisborough firmly found its identity as a market town. The growth of population in this period was slow. Hearth Tax returns for the late 17th century suggest that about a thousand people lived in Guisborough. The 1801 census return gives a population total of 1,719; as well as farm workers, this figure included a number of craftsmen such as weavers, tanners, wheelwrights, masons and blacksmiths, along with a wide cross-section of tradespeople. By the early 19th century, the Market Place had become the centre of coaching activity as well as being the scene of the weekly market. The Buck, the Seven Stars and the Cock Inn (now the National Westminster Bank) were all coaching inns. By 1840 there were daily departures to Stockton and Whitby, and the 'Earl

GUISBOROUGH, *Westgate c1955* G66024

of Zetland' coach ran from the Buck to Redcar on alternate days during the bathing season! Mail came via Thirsk and the Cleveland Tontine. The arrival of the railway in the 1850s was to revolutionise this local scene, as it did throughout the country.

We now move into what is arguably one of the most important periods of Guisborough's history, shaping much of the town as we know it today. The discovery of ironstone in the hills around the town brought Guisborough into the mining boom, which drastically changed the Tees Valley and East Cleveland area. A comparison of the 1851 and the 1861 census returns graphically illustrates the rate of change in the town. In 1851 there were no miners or railway workers here, but by 1861 there were 319 miners and 102 railway workers, and the population of Guisborough had doubled. Small farms and small holdings had been replaced with streets of cottages built at short notice to house the miners and their families; they came from all parts of

the country, in particular from Lincolnshire and East Anglia, attracted here by the prospect of regular work and higher wages. This pattern of street building continued with the growth of the mining industry, and by the end of the 19th century the old north and south back lanes and the medieval strips which linked them had been filled with rows of terraced housing. Inevitably these new streets bore the names of either the mine owners or the developers: examples are Bolckow Street (1875), Walkers Row (1854), Bennison Street (1880), Reid Terrace (1878), and Hedley Street (1885). Reid Terrace and Hedley Street formed part of the town's first housing estate, as they were laid out on the former Sunnyfield Estate in an attempt by a group of Victorian property developers to provide 'a better class of housing'.

The 1860s and 70s saw Guisborough under the patronage of Admiral Thomas Chaloner. After retiring from the regular Navy upon inheriting the Guisborough estate, the admiral threw

GUISBOROUGH *1891* 29208

himself into public life and was a leading figure during an active period in the town's history. In 1873 he endowed the town with a miners' Accident Hospital - the growth of the mines had resulted in the need for treatment from the effects of numerous horrendous accidents. After the formation of the Guisborough School Board in the 1870s, he gave the sites for the new Providence and Northgate schools. In the 1870s he also gave sites for a town cemetery and a Temperance Hall and Mechanics Institute. These last two philanthropic institutions formed part of the admiral's development of a new artery in the town centre connecting Westgate to the newly opened railway station, which he named Chaloner Street. As a Justice of the Peace, Chairman of the Board of Magistrates and Chairman of the Guisborough Board of Health, the admiral oversaw huge improvements to the town, and he was undoubtedly an integral part of the story of Victorian Guisborough.

Whilst mining provided the majority of employment, one significant local enterprise made an important contribution to the economy of Guisborough. In 1861 Mr John Sutherst set up an iron foundry, initially to meet a demand for the repair and maintenance of mining equipment. By the end of the century the company had extended its activities to include the manufacture of steel castings, mainly for the local iron and steel industry. In the early 1900s the business was taken over by Messrs Blackett & Hutton, and it provided employment for generations of men in the town until its closure in the late 20th century.

20th-century Guisborough saw a pattern of rise and decline. The mining industry continued to underpin the town's economy until the mines' closure in the 1930s. The inevitable unemployment levels which followed heralded a bleak period in Guisborough's history, echoing patterns of earlier centuries. Following the Second World War, the continual development of the chemical industry gave Guisborough a life-

HUTTON, *Highcliff and Cleveland Hills c1885* 18145

16

line, for many Guisborough men found employment there. As the chemical giants such as ICI brought personnel from all over the country to work on their sites, Guisborough became a very popular place to live, and it found a new role as a dormitory town. During the 1960s and 70s Guisborough was one of the fastest-growing towns in England; the fields which surrounded the town gave way to the new housing estates which characterise 21st-century Guisborough. Now in the new millennium, Guisborough has witnessed the decline of the chemical and steel industry, and strives to find a new role as it moves into the next chapter of its history.

GUISBOROUGH, *Market Place 1907* 58660

WESTGATE

WESTGATE *1899* 44758

In this delightful and evocative view, we see the north or 'top' side of Westgate. On the extreme left is the watchmaker's and jeweller's shop of George Page, a keen amateur photographer; many of his photographs of events in the town were taken from his first floor drawing room window, shown here, with the distinctive clock below. Like many trades-people in the town, Mr and Mrs Page lived above the shop. Next to Page's we find Mr Simpson, a tobacconist, then Brunton's the pork butchers and Scott's the grain and seed merchants. The gas lamp denotes the post office at number 16 Westgate, and next to it at number 14 we find Mr Franks, a baker's and confectioner's and dining rooms. In 1910 Mr Franks retired and sold the business to Mr Tom Pallister, and the business traded until the early 1960s as simply Pallisters.

▼ **WESTGATE** *1913* 66019

The wide sweep of cobbles and double avenue of trees defines this characteristic view on entering the town from the west. It shows Westgate, the main thoroughfare of the town centre, and leading off to the left is Westgate Road, opened up in 1876 on the site of the former driveway to Sunnyfield House, a prominent private residence in the town. The view is flanked on the right by the Primitive Methodist church, built in 1907 at a cost of £4,000 to replace an earlier chapel in Chapel Street, off Chaloner Street. The private houses on the left are now commercial premises, and the cottages set back a little further along were demolished in the late 1960s to make way for two retail units.

▶ **WESTGATE** *1955* G66037

This is the bottom or western end of Westgate. The fine double avenue of trees, principally horse chestnuts, were originally planted in 1887 to mark Queen Victoria's Golden Jubilee, then mainly re-planted in 1910. The planting of the trees was an imaginative piece of landscaping, and in their full maturity in the mid 20th century they gave tremendous pleasure to residents of the town. In recent years many have died, sad to say, and have been replaced with young saplings. The pair of gates on the right lead to Lower Garth, a significant and much admired private residence.

WESTGATE *1955*
G66028

We are a little further 'up street' - a commonly used Guisborough expression for visiting Westgate. Guisborough has never had a High Street, and Westgate has simply come to be known as 'the Street' or 'the main street'. To the left of the Primitive Methodist chapel can be seen the tiled façade of the King's Head public house, and to the right is the central premises of the Guisborough Provident and Industrial Society or Co-op, opened in 1905 and at its height boasting a covered arcade and a wide range of departments. The central premises were demolished in 1985 to make way for the present-day Safeway/Morrisons development.

WESTGATE *1955* G66016

Cars parked on the cobbles are starting to become a characteristic of Westgate by the mid 1950s, though parking spaces are far more readily found than today! Here we see the north or 'top side' of Westgate, as it is affectionately referred to by Gisborians. Ernie Alcock's fruiterer's shop flanks the left of the view, and further along refreshment can be sought at either the Co-op Snack Bar or Pallister's Café. The shops on the north of Westgate, facing due south, benefit from direct sun, hence the fashion through much of the 20th century for using sun blinds, as we see here.

▶ **WESTGATE** *1955* G66024

Further 'up street' we now meet the junction of Westgate with Chaloner Street, which leads off to the right. Like Westgate Road, Chaloner Street was opened up in Victorian times, in this case in the 1860s to connect the town centre to the recently opened railway station, which served the town until the early 1960s. Mr Thirkell's butcher's shop with its corner door stands at the junction of the two streets (right), and next to it is Westbrook's newsagent's shop (apparently being decorated – note the man on the ladder). From here a pedestrian crossing leads over Westgate to Pallister's baker's shop and café; behind it was their bakehouse, the Priory Hall function room, and the family's private residence, known in the town (not surprisingly and with some affection) as Teacake Villa.

◄ **WESTGATE,** *Sunnyfield House c1960* G66054

Number 36 Westgate, known since the mid 19th century as Sunnyfield House, was built in around 1780 as the residence of John Harrison, agent to the Chaloner estate. The Sunnyfield Estate originally comprised a large area of 'pleasure grounds and grass land' to the north of Westgate. After being sold at auction in 1876, the estate was broken up, and most of the land was developed with private housing. The house (now a Town Council Community Centre), the stable block (now the Town Museum) and the immediate gardens eventually became the home in 1902 of Dr William Stainthorpe, who extended the house in 1919 to provide a private nursing home – the birthplace of many Gisborians from the 1920s through to the early 1950s. The original carriage driveway of the house preceded the 'new' Westgate Road, shown in the foreground here, which was laid out to connect the Victorian streets of Reid Terrace, Gill Street and Hedley Street to the town centre. The original screen or fence in front of Sunnyfield House has been a familiar part of Westgate for over two centuries. Peeping out to the right of the house is the façade of the Wesleyan Methodist chapel, which was built in 1811, remodelled in 1886 and demolished in 1963. The site of the chapel now serves as a car park; pedestrian access to it is still via an opening between numbers 28 and 30 Westgate, the original route to the chapel.

▶ **WESTGATE** *c1960* G66053

By 1960, the pedestrian crossing over Westgate had been moved to its present position, in the foreground of this view. The newly opened post office of 1956 (right) served the town until the late 1990s, when it was sub-divided into three retail units. On the extreme left are the premises of the Trustee Savings Bank - it moved across the road later in the 1960s. In the centre of the view, behind the Market Cross, we see property in the Market Place and entrance to Church Street before it was demolished as part of a road-widening scheme in the early 1960s.

▲ **WESTGATE** *c1965* G66072

Compare this scene with G66053, five years after it but almost identical. By now the impact of the alterations to the Market Place and Church Street of 1962/63 are clear. The Fine Fare Supermarket (extreme left of the picture) has now replaced the Co-op Snack Bar, and although Leemings the chemist (next door) remains, Pallister's cake shop beyond has now become Shipmans, which it remained until the 1990s. On the right, next to the archway is Gray's cycle and pram shop, and beyond that the Chocolate Box and Hintons, the forerunner of the present day Safeway/Morrisons store.

▼ **WESTGATE** *c1965* G66067

More cars on the cobbles are noticeable now. The impressive edifice of the Midland Bank, number 12 Westgate, is second from the left. Built in the late 18th century as the residence of Dr Bird, the house, like Sunnyfield House, had grounds stretching back to the North Bank Lane, now known as Bolckow Street/Park Lane (it was on this land that Mr Tom Pallister, the baker and confectioner, built his Teacake Villa in 1924, the house where the author was born in the year of this photograph). Dr Bird's house became a bank in the late 19th century, and the mock Georgian façade was added in 1919 to promote an image of security and trust. The first and second floors provided a manager's residence for many years, which enjoyed a walled garden to the rear. Next to the bank is Boothroyd's TV and radio shop, and next door but one is the Orange Café, the venue of many a wedding reception, coming of age party and funeral tea in the town.

WESTGATE *c1965* G66074

At the western end of Westgate, we see very clearly how the trees planted at either side of the road created a very attractive avenue effect when entering the town in this direction. On the extreme right is Kemplah House, a private preparatory school run by Miss MacDonald and originally the residence of Mr Clarke. He was a prominent local land agent; his single-storey office can be seen to the left of Kemplah House, still practising at the time of this photograph as Clarke & Watson. New Road, another Victorian street, runs off to the right; at its junction with Westgate we see Wetherall's furniture store, still serving the needs of the town today. On the left, by the Hillman Imp, we see the opening created by the demolition of cottages in the early 1960s to make way for the town's Register Office and Library.

THE MARKET PLACE

MARKET PLACE *1891* 29210

Since medieval times the Market Place has formed a focal point in the town. It is dominated by the early 19th-century market cross, from where John Wesley preached on one of his visits to Guisborough. Between 1876 and 1899 a public urinal stood in the centre of the Market Place – we can see it very clearly in this view. It was eventually moved by order of the Guisborough Board of Health to a more discreet location behind the Town Hall! The distinctive bow windows and buck statue and portico of the Buck Hotel flank the extreme right, while beyond are the chemist's and druggist's shops of Mr Fairburn and Mr Bancks, next door to each other just as today's Boots and Leemings operate side by side further down Westgate. Leemings was the successor of Mr Bancks, moving from the Market Place down into Westgate in 1902.

MARKET PLACE *1891*
29209

A group of smiling boys stand in front of the market cross with its drinking fountain, given to the town by Lady Pease. The two-storey bay window immediately to the right of the cross is a remnant of the Cock Inn, which closed in the 1870s. The majority of the old inn building was converted into a bank, which it remains today, but the section to the left of the arch became a separate shop unit. Next to it we find Metcalfe's, printers, booksellers, stationers and newsagents. The shops occupied here by Jackson (boots and shoes) and Hillary (jewellers, centre) were demolished as part of the widening of Church Street in 1962/63.

MARKET PLACE *1899*
44756

By 1899 we see that the old two-storey bay window of the Cock Inn has gone, to be replaced by a new shop front installed by Mr Fairburn, who had moved his chemist's and druggist's business across the road from the shop we saw in the view of 1891. This shop, which boasted a spiral staircase, remained a chemist's shop for much of the 20th century. Mr Fairburn was famous for his own blend of whisky, known as Abbey Brand (named incorrectly after the priory, which was often referred to by Victorians as the abbey). Since 1891, Mr Hillary has sold his jeweller's shop to Mr Boothroyd (centre right), and the house next to the Buck Hotel, has been replaced with a shop front and the arrival in the town of Walter Willson's 'Smiling Service' (left).

▲ MARKET PLACE 1907
58660

It is market day, and we see traders gathered around the Market Place, traditionally the scene of the market before it moved into Westgate during the second half of the 20th century. A variety of home furnishings - a brass bed, a mattress and a chaise longue - are offered by the market trader, while to the right of the Buck Hotel is the department store of D E Baker, with a grocery department and drapery department. The Baker family were Quakers and are buried in the town's Quaker burial ground behind the present-day library.

▶ *detail of 58660*

THE MARKET CROSS AND WESTGATE *c1955* G66002

This is the north side of the Market Place, looking down into Westgate. On the extreme left is the 19th-century Town Hall, built in two phases, the ground and first floors in 1821 and the second floor in 1870. To the right of the Market Cross we see Branch Number 2 of the Guisborough Provident and Industrial Society - or simply the Co-op. Next to this is Moore's Stores and then Martins Bank; between the two is Dragon Passage, an old right of way, still exercised today through the present day Barclays Bank premises and a remnant from the old George and Dragon Inn, which stood here until the 1920s. Mr Gallante's ice cream is for sale at his parlour at the junction of the Market Place with Northgate - his slogan was: 'when the heat of the day is oppressive, and you're scorched by the sun's golden gleam, then just take a sample of Gallante's delicious ice cream'!

THE MARKET CROSS *1955*
G66010

Further up into the Market Place from G66002, we see the town's library at number 14 Market Place (left) before its move to new premises behind Westgate in the early 1960s. Next door is Arthur Routledge, an auctioneer; beside him, over half a century on from 1899, Walter Willson's service is still smiling on Guisborough. On the extreme right, at number 15 Market Place, is R S Pallister's butcher's shop and at number 17 was Elizabeth's, a ladies' and children's outfitter (just out of picture). Both shops were demolished and rebuilt in a modern style in the early 1970s.

MARKET PLACE *c1965* G66063

It is ten years after G66010, and more cars are evident. This view is flanked on the left by the shop front of Greenwoods chemist's and druggist's shop. We have a splendid view both of the Town Hall and the Market Cross, over the centuries the focal point for the town's New Year's Eve festivities. The area to the right of the cross was laid with cobbles and pedestrianised in a controversial scheme carried out in the late 1990s.

BOW STREET

BOW STREET *1899* 44759

Bow Street runs out of the south side of the Market Place. On the right are some fine trees which formed part of the Priory Gardens until 1967, when the present Church Hall was built. On the left, the pretty double fronted cottage was demolished and rebuilt as a private house in the early 1900s. Next to it we find the three-storey premises - shop and residence - of Mr Wright, a tailor and outfitter, and beyond this a row of cottages and the old Fox Inn, all of which were demolished in 1926 to make way for the present day Fox Inn. We may be thankful that at the time of this rebuilding the old mounting block was retained and repositioned and survives to this day.

THE FOX INN *c1960* G66049

Here we get a splendid view of the frontage of the 1926 Fox Inn building, largely unchanged today. Next to it stands the newsagent's and tobacconist's shop of the Robinson family, who for two generations served the town and, indeed, had their own blend of snuff. The shop was well placed, as passengers bound for their morning train and returning from their evening train passed Robinson's shop for a morning or evening paper. The railway station, which closed in 1963, was situated at the end of Bow Street. At the opposite end of the street is the Seven Stars Inn, which along with the Buck Hotel and the Cock Inn represented the three old coaching inns of Guisborough.

BOW STREET *c1965* G66065

Mr Pallister's butcher's shop flanks the entry to Bow Street. Next to him is Elizabeth's the outfitter's and then Mr Winter's jeweller's shop. All these shops were demolished in the early 1970s to make way for a rather incongruous modern building, which remains today. The entrance to the railway station can just be deciphered in the far distance, with the public conveniences in front, standing at the junction of Bow Street and Fountain Street. Again we see the trees on the east side of the street, home for many years to a thriving rookery. The bow window of the Seven Stars Inn flanks the right of the view.

CHURCH STREET

CHURCH STREET *1891* 29208

We are looking from the tower of the parish church. This panoramic view shows how Church Street connects the Market Place to the church and the priory ruins, with the Victorian street of Redcar Road beyond. The corner shop (with a man standing outside) is the premises of Brice's, painters and decorators. On the next corner we find Mr Bramley, a tailor, who was something of a legend in North Yorkshire, with people coming from far and wide to have their suits made by him. He is commemorated in the parish church by a stained glass window depicting a half-eaten apple - a clever reference to his surname. Opposite Mr Bramley's shop, an old stone trod, or crossing, is clearly shown. On the extreme right we can just see the old theatre in Northgate and the houses on the 'North Back Lane' or Bolckow Street, built in the 1870s by Bolckow Vaughan to house miners. As we see here, they stood in open fields until the land opposite (the Sunnyfield Estate) was developed with housing. Brice's shop and the adjoining cottages were demolished and rebuilt in a similar style in the late 1980s.

CHURCH STREET
1913 66018

D E Baker's department store (extreme left) flanks the entry to Church Street from the Market Place; the road was very much narrower than today, following the road widening scheme and demolition of the property on the right carried out in 1962/63. Richardson's ironmongery shop is further up on the left. Then comes Wear's Café and Barker Brothers (antiques, restoration and cabinet making). The Red Lion Inn beyond was popular with farmers visiting the cattle mart, which lay to the rear, off Patten Lane. On the opposite side is the Abbey Café, named again, incorrectly, after the priory. The window on the extreme right was rescued during the demolition and taken to the Castle Museum in York, where it was incorporated into a reconstructed Victorian street.

▶ THE CHURCH
The Interior 1891 29215

The interior of the parish church is very different today. Although the pews of 1876 (which replaced much earlier box pews) still survive, the majority of the interior was remodelled in a major restoration under the hand of the architect Temple Moore between 1903 and 1908. Before this, as we see here, the walls and nave pillars and arches were plastered and whitewashed. The ceiling was under-drawn, and a three-light window served as the east window and was flanked by boards showing the Ten Commandments. Low pews in the chancel served as choir stalls.

THE PARISH CHURCH

THE CHURCH, *The Interior 1907* 58662

Here we see the extent of the Temple Moore restoration. The walls, pillars and arches have been stripped of plaster, and the under-drawn ceiling has been removed to reveal the impressive chancel arch. New choir stalls have appeared, and whilst the sanctuary had been panelled out and re-floored in 1893, Temple Moore installed a new reredos (now in the church's memorial chapel) and designed a new east window, erected by the Chaloner family in memory of Thomas 'Admiral' Chaloner. A matching window was placed in the tower at the west end in memory of Thomas's widow Amelia, who, along with many of the parishioners of the time, did not unreservedly approve of the major changes to the church which Temple Moore wrought. A new hammer beam roof was installed, but the Victorian pulpit and the Chaloner family box pew (right) were retained. Umbrella stands have been added to the pew ends and gas lighting has been installed.

THE CHURCH, *The De Brus Cenotaph 1899* 44766

The De Brus Cenotaph is the most significant surviving relic of the town's priory. For many years, the two sides of the cenotaph were let into the walls of the church entrance porch, as we see here. One side of the cenotaph depicts the de Brus's of Skelton, the English de Brus's, and the other side the de Brus's of Annandale, the Scottish de Brus's. This view depicts the Scottish side.

THE CHURCH, *The De Brus Cenotaph 1899* 44765

Here we see the English side of the De Brus Cenotaph. The cenotaph was presented to the priory by Margaret Tudor, daughter of Henry VII; it can be dated by the carving second from right, which shows a cock on a reel , a rebus for James Cockerill, penultimate prior of the priory, who was in office at the time when the cenotaph was presented to the priory.

THE CHURCH, *The De Brus Cenotaph 1913* 66010

As part of the Temple Moore restoration of the church, the De Brus Cenotaph was reassembled to look as far as possible as it would have been in the days of the priory. The top had been used for many years as the church's high altar, and indeed the original base still resides in the chancel floor, just in front of the altar step. One end, shown here, had been lying in the priory grounds, but the other end has never been traced. Temple Moore placed the newly assembled cenotaph in the south-west corner, next to the old three-light east window, which was relocated from the sanctuary. The window contains glass from the priory, and in the late 20th century a selection of floor tiles from the priory was placed around the cenotaph, reuniting three significant elements of the priory.

THE CHURCH, *The Font and the Lady Pease Memorial Window 1913* 66009

In the north-west corner, Temple Moore designed a window with tracery to match that of the old three-light east window, which he had relocated to the south-west corner. The window was glazed by the Pease family in memory of Lady Pease of the nearby Hutton and Pinchinthorpe estate. The font in Victorian high Gothic style was given to the church by the Trevor family, solicitors in the town. In 1967, as part of a reorganisation of the church, the font was moved to the north-east corner, and in 1978 this corner was refurbished and dedicated as a memorial chapel in memory of the dead of the town and of two world wars. As a focal point, Temple Moore's reredos, which had been removed from the high altar in 1967, was restored and placed above the altar of the new chapel, where it remains to this day.

THE CHURCH *1913* 66008

This photograph of the west front was taken shortly after completion of the Temple Moore restoration, as we can see from the light-coloured stonework around the window, buttresses and parapets to the left of the tower. The clock had been installed in 1902 as the town's memorial to Queen Victoria, and has always remained something of a peculiarity. As the town or civic clock set in the church building, it is not surprising that there has been much confusion over the years as to who is responsible for its upkeep: is it the Council or the church? The rector of the period, the Rev Cobham, appears to be in conversation with a lady parishioner at the church gate.

THE CHURCH AND THE WAR MEMORIAL *1932* 85336

Comparison with the view of 1913 shows that by 1932 the original diamond-shaped surround to the clock face has been removed, but to this day the marks left by it can be clearly seen on the stonework. Also gone is the gas lamp over the wrought iron gates. Most noticeable by its appearance since 1913 is the town's war memorial or cenotaph, which was erected in 1925 in memory of those who fell in the First World War. The erection of the memorial was largely due to the untiring efforts of the rector of the period, the Rev Mackie, whose memory is perpetuated today in the town's Mackie Drive. The silver birches (left) have grown considerably over the 19 years between the two photographs.

THE PARISH CHURCH AND THE WAR MEMORIAL *c1955* G66006

Here we have the same scene again, 23 years on. The wrought iron railings and gates were removed during the Second World War. As we see here, the large stone gateposts were left standing for a number of years before being removed to give the area in front of the church a more open look. Additional plaques have been added to the war memorial to commemorate those men of the town who fell in the Second World War. The raised area to the left of the church houses the Jackson vault, the resting place of the forebears of the late Adrian Ward Jackson, well known through his friendship with the late Diana, Princess of Wales. The bench in front of it has provided a sunny place for rest and conversation or simply watching the world go by for generations of Gisborians. The gateway on the extreme right leads to the priory ruins.

THE CHURCH *c1955* G66034

This is the east end of the church. In the 1870s the churchyard became quite literally full up, and in consequence Admiral Chaloner gave a site on the eastern outskirts of the town for use as a cemetery. Thereafter, the only interments in the churchyard were those of family members into existing family graves. For ease of maintenance, the headstones no longer mark the positions of the graves and now stand in uniform rows. The churchyard contains some significant tabletop tombs, and also a memorial to John Walker Ord, author of 'Ord's History of Cleveland', regarded for many years as the definitive history of the Cleveland area. This view shows clearly the vestry block (to the right of the chancel) which was added in the 1880s.

THE PRIORY RUINS AND PRIORY GARDENS

THE PRIORY *1885* 18151

The priory was founded in 1119, rebuilt after a disastrous fire and then closed during Henry VIII's Dissolution of the Monasteries. The priory ruins, and in particular the east end, have become synonymous with Guisborough, appearing on many civic documents and motifs and majestically looking over the town and its people for generations with an almost benevolent and reassuring steadfastness. The survival of the east end was largely due to the 18th-century fashion for landscaped parks and follies; the Chaloner family retained and enhanced the Priory Arch, as it is often referred to in town. In this now almost classic view, we see that a Victorian greenhouse once stood in front of the arch (right); judging by its chimneystack, it was presumably heated. Directly in front of the Priory Arch we see the old font of the parish church, which was replaced in the 1870s by the present Trevor font. The old font was moved into the priory grounds, where it remained for many years.

► THE PRIORY c1885 18153

In Victorian times the priory was often incorrectly referred to as 'the abbey', and this led to considerable confusion. Many souvenirs and postcards of the late 19th and early 20th centuries bear the legend 'the abbey'. This unusual view shows the priory arch from the south; in the foreground are gardens which became a formal rose garden laid out for Margaret, later the first Lady Gisborough (see photograph 54863). The clump of trees to the right of the picture are the Monks' Walk, and above the paling fence is the wall of the Long Terrace. A flight of steps from this terrace led up to the priory ruins and was flanked by two carved demi-sea wolves, the crest of the Chaloner family. Gisborians mistakenly thought that these creatures were dragons, and hence the steps became known as the Dragon Steps.

◄ THE MONKS' WALK c1885 18155

This oval-shaped double avenue of lime trees was laid out by the Chaloner family in the 18th century. In the centre was a manicured lawn that in latter years was often the venue for musical and theatrical productions. Although now overgrown, the Monks' Walk still exists, and those of a more superstitious nature perpetuate the legend of the walk being haunted by the ghost of a monk from the days of the nearby priory.

THE PRIORY 1891 29213

Again we still see the old font in front of the priory arch and a gravel path to the right, long since disappeared, which presumably led to the greenhouse shown in the view of 1885. Visible here are the two stone coffins which for many years have stood at the base of the arch, and also the entrances to the two stone spiral staircases which lead up to the window at the very top of the arch, across which many an intrepid Gisborian claims to have walked before the bottoms of the staircases were removed for reasons of safety. The high stone wall to the left has always afforded the priory grounds with privacy and protection; the grounds have a 'secret garden' quality, and their tranquillity and peace are in sharp contrast to the hustle and bustle of the nearby town centre. There is a panoramic view from the arch across the adjoining farmland and Applegarth towards Gisborough Hall. This view was enhanced as part of the Chaloners' landscaping in the 18th century when the tracery of the former east window was removed to afford this fine prospect.

PRIORY GARDENS 1899 44761

Here we see the priory ruins viewed from the south as in the view of 1885; but by the time of this photograph, Margaret, later first Lady Gisborough, along with her head gardener, Kew-trained James Bourne, have begun laying out a series of formal gardens. Flanked by elaborate (and labour intensive!) bedding schemes, typical of the late Victorian and Edwardian period, a gravelled path led to the Monks' Walk and the old chestnut tree (in the clump of trees to the right of the priory arch, and see 44769). The path also led to the Dragon Steps (just visible on the left) and on to the Long Terrace and thence into the priory ruins themselves.

▼ PRIORY GARDENS *1899* 44769

Within the priory grounds, close to the Monks' Walk, there was a very old chestnut tree, believed to be one of the largest in England. The tree was a much visited feature of the town, particularly by generations of Guisborough school children; they were taken there by their teachers, who often got the children to link arms around the girth of the tree (which was considerable) to illustrate its age. As we can see in this photograph, some of the heavy lower branches of the tree eventually touched the ground and took root, creating a ring of younger trees around the venerable parent!

▶ THE OLD GATEWAY *1906*
54866

Often referred to in the town as the Norman arch, the ruined former gateway to the priory stands in Church Street and looks much today as it appears on this view. The large outer arched gateway leads to a pair of arches: the larger, on the left, is for vehicles, and the smaller, on the right, for pedestrians. The structural support section on the vehicular arch we see in this view has long since disappeared, presumably bearing witness to the structural integrity of the arch and the skills of the stonemasons who built it.

◀ **THE PRIORY**
The Rose Garden
1906 54863

Part of a series of gardens laid out by Margaret, later the first Lady Gisborough, the rose garden afforded picturesque views of the neighbouring priory ruins. In the early 20th century, the immaculately kept Priory Gardens were, for a small fee, open to the people of the town, to whom they represented a great amenity. In addition to the rose garden, there was a sunken Italian garden, with an ornamental pool in its centre. In the years before the Second World War, the Priory Gardens were entered by a picturesque gateway in Bow Street.

▶ **THE PRIORY AND THE LAKE** *1932*
85330

The Monks' Pond (or lake) lies to the south east of the priory ruins on Whitby Lane. Screened from the road by rhododendrons, the Monks' Pond creates a very dramatic appearance as it reflects the priory arch - a frequent inspiration over the years for artists and photographers, including Francis Frith and Co. Twenty-four years earlier, in 1908, the Monks' Pond was the scene of an elaborate water tableau held to raise money for the Temple Moore restoration of the parish church. Organised by Margaret Chaloner, later first Lady Gisborough, the story of the tableau is recounted in a privately published account by one of her daughters, entitled 'My Mother's Dream'; it describes vividly the scenes from Greek mythology and the Arthurian legends which were acted out to great effect on the lake.

THE PRIORY *1932* 85329

In this dramatic view, we see the east end of the priory ruins viewed from the east, an area commonly referred to in the town as the Applegarth. Immediately to the east of the priory arch is a well kept lawn, known as the East Lawn - a venue for dances during the grand bazaars and garden fetes held in the priory grounds in the early years of the 20th century. Beyond the East Lawn lies a ha-ha to keep cattle out of the priory grounds. The clump of trees to the left of the priory arch is the Monks' Walk.

THE GRAMMAR SCHOOL

GUISBOROUGH GRAMMAR SCHOOL *1891* 29211

In 1887 the Board of Governors of the newly reconstituted Guisborough Grammar School commissioned Alfred Waterhouse, an eminent Victorian architect, most famous for designing the Natural History Museum in London, to design the new Grammar School buildings and the headmaster's house (right), seen here shortly after their completion. The Chairman of the Board of Governors was Sir Joseph Whitwell Pease; twenty years earlier, he had used Alfred Waterhouse to design his mansion, Hutton Hall, and one assumes this connection influenced the choice of architect for the Grammar School buildings. Built in Waterhouse's characteristic red brick and terracotta style, the buildings replaced the old almshouses and school buildings that fronted Church Walk. The plaque over the central archway reads: 'Guisborough Grammar School - founded in the reign of Queen Elizabeth AD 1561, re-erected in the reign of Queen Victoria AD 1887'.

GUISBOROUGH
GRAMMAR SCHOOL *1899*
44768

In 1899 the Board of Governors of the Grammar School commissioned the building of a library at the western end of the school buildings (left). In the foreground we see the railings of both the school and the churchyard of the parish church, both of which were removed during the collection of wrought iron in the Second World War. The spire or turret on the roof of the school was removed in 1919 and replaced with a clock in memory of the old boys of the school who fell in the First World War.

GUISBOROUGH GRAMMAR SCHOOL *1932* 85335

Now we can see the clock erected in memory of the old boys who had lost their lives in the First World War. At around the time of this photograph, Guisborough received a visit from Prince George, later Duke of Kent, who lost his life in a mysterious air crash during the Second World War; he went to the Grammar School, where he planted a tree. In 1994, his daughter-in-law, the present Duchess of Kent, visited the school, by now the Prior Pursglove Sixth Form College, to open the new Pursglove Centre. It is a strange coincidence that the only two royal visits to Guisborough were made by the same branch of our royal family and to the same building in the town.

THE APPLEGARTH

THE GRAMMAR SCHOOL *c1955* G66012

This attractive view of the Grammar School buildings was taken from the Applegarth, flanked on the right by a copse of pine trees, still standing today. The Applegarth path in the foreground, with kissing gates at either end, connects Church Walk to Whitby Lane, and has always been a favourite walk for Gisborians. Just to the right of the headmaster's house we can see the Coverdale or Jubilee range of buildings, built in 1935, the year of George V's Silver Jubilee.

THE APPLEGARTH *c1955* G66011

This view was taken in the same year as G66012 from the opposite end of the Applegarth at Whitby Lane, with the kissing gates in the foreground. Without doubt, this is one of the loveliest views in Guisborough, beloved of many Gisborians, and not least the author; the juxtaposition of the priory arch and the parish church is remarkable, with the former literally framing the latter. The Monks' Pond, scene of the water tableau of 1908, is located just to the left of the view. To the right, Whitby Lane leads to Gisborough Hall.

GISBOROUGH HALL

LONG HULL *1891* 29217

In the 1850s Admiral Thomas Chaloner retired from the regular navy and along with his wife Amelia took up residence on the Gisborough estate, which he had inherited. In 1857 the admiral chose a commanding south-facing site on Whitby Lane and commissioned Teulon, a distinguished architect of the time, to build him a new residence in the domestic Gothic style. The new house, named Long Hull (meaning long field, a reference to the land on which the house was built) included quirky architectural references to the admiral's naval career, most notably the oriel bay window above the entrance door, which was built to resemble the stern of a ship, with a porthole window to its side. The stone balustrading in the foreground and the monkey puzzle tree on the extreme right have long since disappeared.

◀ GISBOROUGH HALL *1907*
58664

Following the death of Admiral Chaloner's widow, Amelia, in 1902, the Gisborough estate was inherited by Richard Godolphin Hume Chaloner, later created First Lord or Baron Gisborough. In 1904 Richard Chaloner commissioned an extensive programme of remodelling and extension of Long Hull, which was renamed Gisborough Hall, the name we know it by today. Comparison of this view of Gisborough Hall's south front with that of Long Hull in 1891 shows clearly the extent of the alterations and extensions, which are particularly apparent by the areas of light-coloured stonework. As part of the same programme of alterations, two lodges or gatehouses were built, one at the end of the south drive and the other at the end of the north drive.

▶ GISBOROUGH HALL
1907 58665

Another view of the south front shows the extent of the alterations and extensions carried out by Richard Chaloner and his wife Margaret, who was also instrumental in the laying out of the Priory Gardens and in organising the water tableau of 1908. The fine lawn in front of the house was often the venue for tennis tournaments in the inter-war period, and the fine copper beech tree (right) still stands. On the official adoption by the Guisborough Urban District Council of the spelling of the town's name as Guisborough, the Chaloner family elected to retain the old spelling of Gisborough, which remains in use for the holder of the Baronage and anything appertaining to the Gisborough estate, including Gisborough Hall.

◄ **GISBOROUGH HALL**
c1955 G66015

By the 1950s the south front of Gisborough Hall was covered in Boston ivy; it still is today, and looks stunning in the autumn. Shortly after this view was taken, the present Lord Gisborough, grandson of Richard and Margaret Chaloner, decided to move out of Gisborough Hall, which was then used as an old people's home. After the building of a purpose-built home in another part of the town, Gisborough Hall was turned into a restaurant, and following a recent major refurbishment and extension project, it now operates as a luxury hotel.

► **HUTTON**
Highcliffe and the Cleveland Hills c1885
18145

The neighbouring estate to the Chaloners' Gisborough estate, the Hutton and Pinchinthorpe estate, was bought in the 1860s by the Quaker industrialist, Joseph Whitwell Pease of Darlington. He commissioned the renowned Victorian architect, Alfred Waterhouse (who designed the Natural History Museum in London) to design a new mansion, Hutton Hall, which was completed in 1867; it replaced a much older house, whose foundations can still be traced today. After the completion of Hutton Hall, Sir Joseph set about landscaping the park surrounding the Hall and the nearby village, introducing specimen trees from many parts of the world, many of which survive today, adding enormously to the character of the Hutton area. Sir Joseph had his own private railway station close by at Hutton Gate, and he laid out an imposing driveway to the Hall to mark his son's 21st birthday, known today as the Avenue. The Hutton and Pinchinthorpe estate was sold by auction and split up in 1902 following the collapse of the Pease's business empire, and the Hall was bought by J W Pickering, a prosperous ship owner.

HUTTON

HUTTON, *The Hall c1885* 18143

Here we see Hutton Hall from the north, showing the main entrance and driveway, the view that house party guests would first see upon arriving by carriage, having been brought up from the Pease's nearby private station. To the right, the rhododendron-lined main driveway leads up from the picturesque lodge or gatehouse, also designed by Waterhouse. To the left, the back drive leads to the turreted courtyard on the extreme left of the Hall and then on to the stables, coach houses and garden buildings.

▼ **HUTTON,** *The Hall 1891* 29218

This is the impressive south front with its conservatory and orangery. Waterhouse favoured the use of contrasting red brick and terracotta; as well as using it at Hutton Hall, he used it on his other two buildings in Guisborough, the Grammar School and Overbeck, a private house on the western outskirts. The elaborate (and labour intensive) formal gardens were very much in the style of the day, and required an army of full-time gardeners. The head gardener and his staff were accommodated in a purpose-built and elaborate range of houses, bothies, potting sheds and greenhouses (together with the adjoining stable block, these were converted in the early years of this century into a luxury development, Pease Court). There was a fernery, an orangery and a grotto, and the size of the head gardener's house, with its back stairs and maids' accommodation, illustrates the size of the household and the importance of the head gardener in the social structure of a grand Victorian country house. The head gardener's house was designed with an angled window so that all his staff could be monitored, and a special path and gate was provided to allow Lady Pease to carry out her weekly inspection of the gardens and greenhouses with the head gardener.

▶ **HUTTON**
The Hall 1891
29219

The well kept lawn is ideal for croquet or other similar genteel leisurely Victorian pastimes.

◄ **HUTTON**, *The Hall, the Waterfall 1891* 29221

Hutton Hall was set in extensive parkland with many focal points such as the waterfall, shown here. In its heyday the parkland also contained a boating lake with boat house and summer houses and tea houses, all strategically placed for guests and members of the family to pause and take rest and refreshment on their perambulations of the estate.

▼ **HUTTON**, *The Village 1891* 29220

Often referred to as 'the Alpine village' because of its sylvan setting at the head of a wooded valley, the cluster of houses known as Hutton Village dates from the mid 19th century, when Mr Thomas, a local mine owner, built two rows of cottages and a row of managers' houses to house the workers in his nearby mine. At that time the village was known as Thomas Town. After the Hutton estate was bought by Joseph Whitwell Pease in the 1860s, the two rows of cottages were prettified by the addition of decorative porches. Sir Joseph built a mission house to cater for the religious needs of the occupants of the houses and cottages, who by this time were estate workers, keeping the extensive Hutton estate in pristine condition. Further down the park, Sir Joseph built a school for the children on the estate, and this establishment, which had an excellent reputation, was also patronised by Guisborough parents.

HUTTON, *The Village 1891* 29220A

This similar view of the village gives a closer impression of the mission house and the row of managers' houses (right). Number 20 Hutton Village, the house on the left-hand end of the terrace, was extended during the early years of the 20th century and almost doubled in size. Between the road leading up to the mission house and the track forking off to the left of it, lies the village green, very much the heart of the village and a place where generations of village children have played, and continue to enjoy many happy hours. For many years the green was dominated by a large tree with a low branch which many generations of village children had fun sitting upon. Some of the sapling trees and conifers shown on the green in this view still stand today. The mission house remained a place of worship well into the 20th century; it was under the pastoral care of the rector of Guisborough, and he or one of his curates came up to the village to hold services there. The author's grandmother was a Sunday School teacher at the mission house in the 1930s, 40s and 50s; she lived in one of the cottages in the village, and here the author's mother was born and brought up.

GIFTS TO THE TOWN FROM ADMIRAL THOMAS CHALONER

THE COTTAGE HOSPITAL *1899* 44762

As the ironstone mines grew in the town in the 1870s and 80s, there were an increasing number of accidents. In response to this, a Matron Stone established a small miners' accident hospital in a cottage at the southern end of New Road. Shortly afterwards, Admiral Thomas Chaloner magnanimously gave the site for and funded the building of a purpose-built miners' accident hospital on Whitby Lane. Completed in 1873, the hospital was later re-named the Admiral Chaloner Hospital to commemorate the admiral's generosity to the town. On the central gable is the date 1873, together with the demi-sea wolf, the crest of the Chaloner family, and the initials of the Admiral (TC) and his wife Amelia (AC). As the mines wound down, the hospital became a cottage hospital for the town, known as the Admiral Chaloner Cottage Hospital or simply the Chaloner, as it was affectionately referred to by Gisborians. In this form the hospital continued to serve the town right up to its closure in the early 1980s, by which time an operating theatre and X-ray facility had been added to the right-hand end of the building. Built in 1928, this addition to the hospital was funded by a scheme organised by Dr W W Stainthorpe, and was notable for being the first X-ray facilities in the town. On the extreme left is a picturesque summer house for convalescent patients, and also the original picturesque footbridge over Chapel Beck to the front entrance of the hospital. At the time of writing (2004), the building (which since 1984 had been used as the premises of Studio Print), was being converted into luxury apartments - another phase in the building's long history of service to the town.

65

THE CEMETERY *1899* 44767

As we leave the town in an easterly direction towards Skelton, our last view of Guisborough, and the resting place of generations of Gisborians since being opened in 1872, is the town's cemetery. After the churchyard became full, Admiral Chaloner gave land for the creation of a new town cemetery, although the churchyard continued to be used for later interments into existing family graves. Laid out in the style of the day, the cemetery had a lodge for the resident cemetery superintendent, a mortuary chapel for the coffins to rest in before the funeral, and two chapels for the holding of funeral services, one Anglican and one Non-conformist. All four cemetery buildings were set in well kept lawned burial areas, punctuated with a gridwork of symmetrical paths and attractive topiary; the cemetery was bounded by a stone wall with wrought iron railings. After falling into disuse, one of the chapels was demolished. The remaining three buildings still stand, but the vehicular gateway shown in this view has been moved from Church Lane to the frontage on the B1269 road to Dunsdale and Redcar.

LOCAL LANDMARKS

HIGHCLIFFE *1913* 66021

All generations of Gisborians feel a spiritual affinity with Highcliffe, which, like an old friend, looks over the town, familiar and steadfast. Fine views of the town are afforded from its summit. The fields in the foreground of this view and Sparrow Lane were a favourite Sunday afternoon walk for the townspeople, and gave way in the 1960s and 1970s to the Hunters Hill and Kemplah Park housing estates. The haymaking shown here is a far cry from the densely packed housing which occupies this land today.

▶ **HIGHCLIFFE** *1913*
66020

Highcliffe's immediate neighbour to the right has always been known in the town as Green Hill, a distinct hillock with a rocky outcrop on its northern face. The hill was forested after World War II by the Forestry Commission and now looks very different from this view. The three-cornered field at the foot of Green Hill was always a familiar spot to the people of the town. This and the preceding view illustrate very graphically why Gisborians have always considered themselves country dwellers: the town is immediately surrounded by fields and hills, nestling in a picturesque valley between the Cleveland and Eston hills.

◀ **ROSEBERRY TOPPING** *c1885*
18147

Often referred to affectionately as 'Cleveland's Matterhorn', the distinctive profile of Roseberry Topping lies a short distance to the west of Guisborough, between Pinchinthorpe and Great Ayton. The walk to its summit has been a popular pastime for generations, and the ascent is well rewarded by breathtaking views in all directions.

▲ **ROSEBERRY TOPPING** *c1885* 18148

At the foot of Roseberry Topping is the hamlet of Newton under Roseberry, and in this view we see the Kings Head Inn (extreme right). To this day it continues to provide a much welcomed place of rest and refreshment following an expedition to the top of Roseberry Topping and back.

◄ **ROSEBERRY TOPPING AND THE KINGS HEAD** *c1960* R54059

It is seventy-five years on from view 18148, and the scene is little changed other than a slight realignment of the track in the foreground, which leads to the centre of the village of Newton under Roseberry. Shortly after this picture was taken, a number of individual private residences were built to the left on what were, without doubt, prime sites commanding superb views of Roseberry Topping.

▶ **GREAT AYTON**
The Bridge and Church Street c1955 G112016

The stone bridge in the foreground crosses the River Leven, which flows through the picturesque village of Great Ayton. The spire of the parish church peeps over the rooftops, and at Walter Willson's grocery shop (right), corned beef can be purchased for 2/8d.

◀ **GREAT AYTON**
High Green c1960
G112022

The Royal Oak has for many years been a favourite hostelry in Great Ayton, and remains so today. It stands in a parade of shops that overlooks the picturesque High Green. Next to the Royal Oak we see the shops of two long established Ayton families, T H Petch, a grocer, and Worthy Pearson, a tobacconist.

THE SURROUNDING TOWNS AND VILLAGES

▼ **GREAT AYTON,** *High Street c1955* G112032

In the High Street we find, amongst other shops, another branch of Worthy Pearson, known in the village as 'bottom Worthys' as opposed to 'top Worthys', the branch shown in photograph G112022.

▶ **GREAT AYTON**
Waterfall Terrace
c1965 G112028

The bridge in the foreground of this photograph leads over the River Leven to a car park designated for the use of patrons of Suggitts ice cream parlour, something of an institution in the village, which remains as popular today as ever.

◀ **UPLEATHAM**
The Church 1923
74251

In the beautiful valley which lies between Guisborough and Saltburn, we find the hamlet of Upleatham and this delightful tiny church. The church was built in 1684, but the majority of the building was demolished in 1822 leaving this tiny building, which remains an integral part of the landscape today.

▲ **UPLEATHAM,** *The Hall c1885* 18141

This fine building, residence of the Earl of Zetland, suffered from land subsidence and had to be demolished, sad to say. Only the gateposts of the drive to this impressive edifice remain.

◄ **KIRKLEATHAM HALL** *c1885* 18138

Another 'lost house' of the East Cleveland area is Kirkleatham Hall. Only the stable block of this building now remains.

KIRKLEATHAM
*The Church
and the Mausoleum
c1885* 18136

The distinctive mausoleum which is attached to the side of St Cuthbert's Church was erected by the Turner family, who owned the Kirkleatham estate and founded the hospital shown in view 18137.

◄ **KIRKLEATHAM**
The Hospital
c1885 18137

Founded by Sir
William Turner with
accommodation for
both elderly men
and women, this
beautiful building,
which survives
almost unchanged
to this day, comprises
two wings of
almshouses which
flank an exquisite
chapel designed
by Sir Christopher
Wren - a real gem.

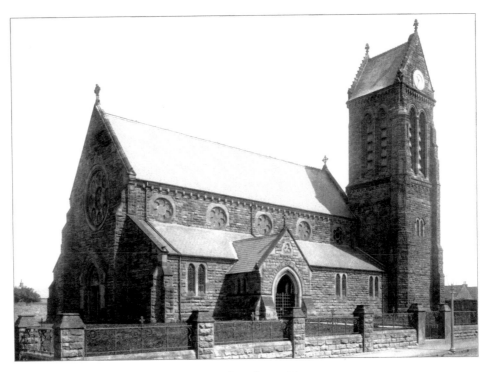

▲ **MARSKE-BY-THE-SEA,** *The New Church c1885* 18127

The parish church of St Mark was built in 1867. In this view we see the shape of the original
tower of the church, which was damaged by fire in 1902 and rebuilt by the Marquis of Zetland.

◄ **MARSKE-BY-
THE-SEA**
Redcar Road 1906
54841

Here we see the tower
of the church after the
rebuilding works,
showing the change
that was made to the
architectural style
of the top of the tower.
The shops in the
foreground include a
grocer's on the corner,
and next to it is a
barber's shop with its
distinctive pole.

▶ **MARSKE-BY-THE-SEA**
High Street 1906
54842

This picturesque view of the High Street is flanked by the Methodist chapel on the left-hand side, now converted into residential units.

◀ **MARSKE-BY-THE-SEA**
The Sands 1906
54847

In this view of Marske beach, with the distinctive cliffs of Huntcliffe in the distance, there appears to be some form of camp being held on the sands with a row of distinctive wigwam-like tents.

▲ **MARSKE-BY-THE-SEA,** *The Slipway and the Sands 1938* 88393

The row of houses on the left-hand side are known as Cliff Terrace; they look across the sands and coastline towards Saltburn. In 1938, visitors to the beach could park their car at the bottom of the slipway for 6d.

◀ **SALTBURN-BY-THE-SEA**
Huntcliffe 1891
29194

The impressive sweep of Saltburn's beach with Huntcliffe overlooking it remains as breathtaking a view today as we see it here in 1891. The whitewashed building overlooking the sea is the Ship Inn, one of the oldest buildings in Saltburn.

SALTBURN-BY-THE-SEA, *Skelton Beck 1891* 29205

In this charming picture there appears to be great hilarity as our Victorian forebears, in full-length dresses, attempt to cross Skelton Beck, picking their way over the precarious rocks.

SALTBURN-BY-THE-SEA, *The Pier 1913* 66358

The pier, one of the few surviving Victorian piers in the country, has recently undergone extensive restoration. It is now shorter than we see it here, as its extremities were swept away by the ferocity of the North Sea. At the head of the pier we can see the cliff lift, still operating today, transporting passengers from the town down to the sea front.

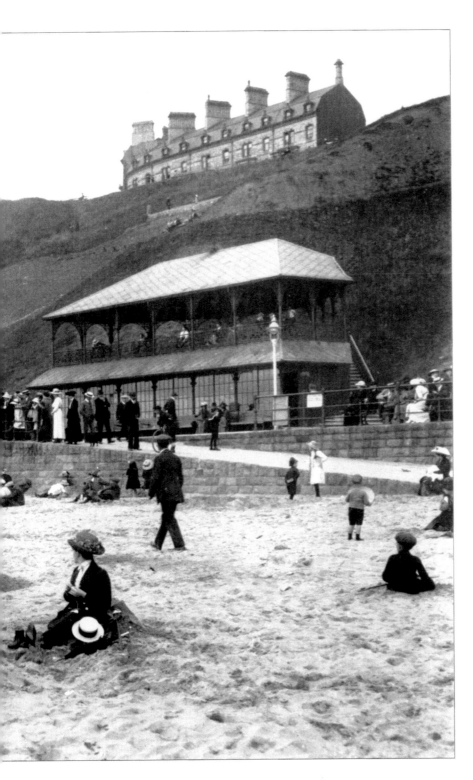

SALTBURN-BY-THE-SEA, *The Sands 1913*
66365

With the British seaside holiday at its heyday, here we see Saltburn beach full of happy holidaymakers, including a crowd of people who appear to be watching some form of entertainment, possibly a Punch and Judy show or pierrots.

81

▶ **SALTBURN-BY-THE-SEA**
The Promenade 1923 74267

People are strolling along the Promenade at Saltburn, just as they do today, to take in the sea air. In the foreground of the picture we see some fascinating early cars, with a chauffeur attending to the needs of his passengers in the car to the right of the picture.

◀ **SALTBURN-BY-THE-SEA**, *The Queens Hotel 1932* 85282

Here we see the impressive edifice of the Queens Hotel, built in 1875 to cater for the large number of tourists who came to Saltburn for their holidays in the late Victorian period. In the centre of the photograph we see the entrance to the railway station, again bringing holidaymakers to the town from different parts of the country.

◄ **SKELTON**
The Church c1885 18125

The parish church of Skelton, built in Victorian times, is dominated by a very large tower, which is something of a landmark in the East Cleveland area.

▼ **SKELTON,** *The Castle 1891* 29207

Skelton Castle, the residence of the Wharton family, owners of the Skelton and Gilling estate, was built in 1794 in the Gothic style and replaced a much earlier castle.

► **SKELTON**
West End c1955 S285011

The West End of Skelton is arranged around the green, where the war memorial stands. This green is flanked by North Terrace, East Terrace, South Terrace and West Terrace.

◄ **SKELTON**
High Street c1955
S285001

The broad High Street of Skelton is flanked on the right by a row of houses which were built for and remain in the ownership of the Skelton and Gilling estate. The large tower of the parish church dominates the centre of the view. Many of the houses on the left-hand side of the street are now commercial premises.

► **SKELTON**
From the Hills c1965 S285030

This photograph was taken from an area of Skelton known as the hills, an area of high ground to the south of the village. From here there are breathtaking views both to the coast and, as seen here, across towards Guisborough.

SKELTON
Church Lane c1965
S285026

Church Lane leads to the entrance to Skelton Castle and also to the old church, which was erected in 1785. After closing in 1904, it stood empty for many years, but it has been lovingly restored and is now back in use.

SKELTON, *The Castle Gardens c1965* S285024

Skelton Castle stands in beautiful grounds. Here we see the old moat, which was landscaped and, as shown here, included an elaborate enclosed formal rose garden.

INDEX

FRITH PRODUCTS & SERVICES

Francis Frith would doubtless be pleased to know that the pioneering publishing venture he started in 1860 still continues today. Over a hundred and forty years later, The Francis Frith Collection continues in the same innovative tradition and is now one of the foremost publishers of vintage photographs in the world. Some of the current activities include:

INTERIOR DECORATION

Today Frith's photographs can be seen framed and as giant wall murals in thousands of pubs, restaurants, hotels, banks, retail stores and other public buildings throughout the country. In every case they enhance the unique local atmosphere of the places they depict and provide reminders of gentler days in an increasingly busy and frenetic world.

PRODUCT PROMOTIONS

Frith products are used by many major companies to promote the sales of their own products or to reinforce their own history and heritage. Frith promotions have been used by Hovis bread, Courage beers, Scots Porage Oats, Colman's mustard, Cadbury's foods, Mellow Birds coffee, Dunhill pipe tobacco, Guinness, and Bulmer's Cider.

GENEALOGY AND FAMILY HISTORY

As the interest in family history and roots grows world-wide, more and more people are turning to Frith's photographs of Great Britain for images of the towns, villages and streets where their ancestors lived; and, of course, photographs of the churches and chapels where their ancestors were christened, married and buried are an essential part of every genealogy tree and family album.

FRITH PRODUCTS

All Frith photographs are available Framed or just as Mounted Prints and Posters (size 23 x 16 inches). These may be ordered from the address below. Other products available are - Address Books, Calendars, Jigsaws, Canvas Prints, Postcards and local and prestige books.

THE INTERNET

Already ninety thousand Frith photographs can be viewed and purchased on the internet through the Frith websites and a myriad of partner sites.

For more detailed information on Frith products, look at this site:
www.francisfrith.com

See the complete list of Frith Books at: www.francisfrith.com
This web site is regularly updated with the latest list of publications from The Francis Frith Collection. If you wish to buy books relating to another part of the country that your local bookshop does not stock, you may purchase on-line.

For further information, trade, or author enquiries please contact us at the address below:
The Francis Frith Collection, Unit 6, Oakley Business Park, Wylye Road, Dinton, Wiltshire SP3 5EU.
Tel: +44 (0)1722 716 376 Fax: +44 (0)1722 716 881 Email: sales@francisfrith.co.uk

---

See Frith products on the internet at www.francisfrith.com

FREE PRINT OF YOUR CHOICE
CHOOSE A PHOTOGRAPH FROM THIS BOOK
+ £3.80 POSTAGE

Mounted Print
Overall size 14 x 11 inches (355 x 280mm)

TO RECEIVE YOUR FREE PRINT

Choose any Frith photograph in this book

Simply complete the Voucher opposite and return it with your remittance for £3.50 (to cover postage and handling) and we will print the photograph of your choice in SEPIA (size 11 x 8 inches) and supply it in a cream mount ready to frame (overall size 14 x 11 inches).

Order additional Mounted Prints
at HALF PRICE - £12.00 each (normally £24.00)

If you would like to order more Frith prints from this book, possibly as gifts for friends and family, you can buy them at half price (with no additional postage costs).

Have your Mounted Prints framed

For an extra £20.00 per print you can have your mounted print(s) framed in an elegant polished wood and gilt moulding, overall size 16 x 13 inches (no additional postage required).

IMPORTANT!

❶ Please note: aerial photographs and photographs with a reference number starting with a "Z" are not Frith photographs and cannot be supplied under this offer.

❷ Offer valid for delivery to one UK address only.

❸ These special prices are only available if you use this form to order. You must use the ORIGINAL VOUCHER on this page (no copies permitted). We can only despatch to one UK address.

❹ This offer cannot be combined with any other offer.

As a customer your name & address will be stored by Frith but not sold or rented to third parties. Your data will be used for the purpose of this promotion only.

Send completed Voucher form to:

**The Francis Frith Collection,
19 Kingsmead Business Park, Gillingham,
Dorset SP8 5FB**

Voucher for **FREE** *and Reduced Price Frith Prints*

Please do not photocopy this voucher. Only the original is valid, so please fill it in, cut it out and return it to us with your order.

Picture ref no	Page no	Qty	Mounted @ £12.00	Framed + £20.00	Total Cost £
		1	Free of charge*	£	£
			£12.00	£	£
			£12.00	£	£
			£12.00	£	£
			£12.00	£	£
			£12.00	£	£

Please allow 28 days for delivery. Offer available to one UK address only

* Post & handling		£3.80
Total Order Cost		£

Title of this book . . . .

I enclose a cheque/postal order for £ . . . .
made payable to 'The Francis Frith Collection'

OR please debit my Mastercard / Visa / Maestro card, details below

Card Number:

Issue No (Maestro only):   Valid from (Maestro):

Card Security Number: Expires:

Signature:

Name Mr/Mrs/Ms . . . .

Address . . . .

. . . .

. . . .

. . . . Postcode . . . .

Daytime Tel No . . . .

Email . . . .

Valid to 31/12/18

Can you help us with information about any of the Frith photographs in this book?

We are gradually compiling an historical record for each of the photographs in the Frith archive. It is always fascinating to find out the names of the people shown in the pictures, as well as insights into the shops, buildings and other features depicted.

If you recognize anyone in the photographs in this book, or if you have information not already included in the author's caption, do let us know. We would love to hear from you, and will try to publish it in future books or articles.

An Invitation from The Francis Frith Collection to Share Your Memories

The 'Share Your Memories' feature of our website allows members of the public to add personal memories relating to the places featured in our photographs, or comment on others already added. Seeing a place from your past can rekindle forgotten or long held memories. Why not visit the website, find photographs of places you know well and add YOUR story for others to read and enjoy? We would love to hear from you!

www.francisfrith.com/memories

Our production team

Frith books are produced by a small dedicated team at offices near Salisbury. Most have worked with the Frith Collection for many years. All have in common one quality: they have a passion for the Frith Collection.

Frith Books and Gifts

We have a wide range of books and gifts available on our website utilising our photographic archive, many of which can be individually personalised.

www.francisfrith.com